W9-AES-989

Who Are the Muslims?
Where Muslims Live, and How They Are Governed

Introducing Islam

Who Are the Muslims?
Where Muslims Live, and How They Are Governed

Melissa S. Carr

Produced by OTTN Publishing, Stockton, New Jersey

Mason Crest Publishers
370 Reed Road
Broomall, PA 19008
www.masoncrest.com

First printing

1 3 5 7 9 8 6 4 2

Library of Congress Cataloging-in-Publication Data

Carr, Melissa S.
  Who are the Muslims? / Melissa S. Carr.
      v. cm. — (Introducing Islam)
Includes bibliographical references and index.
  ISBN 1-59084-701-6
1. Islam—Juvenile literature. 2. Muslims—Juvenile literature.
3. Civilization, Islamic—Juvenile literature. 4. Islamic
countries—Civilization—Juvenile literature. [1. Islam. 2. Muslims.
3. Civilization, Islamic. 4. Islamic countries—Civilization.] I. Title.
II. Series.
  BP161.3.C37 2004
  297'.09—dc22

                              2003013297

Contents

Introduction

The central belief of Islam, one of the world's major religions, is contained in a simple but powerful phrase: "There is no god but Allah, and Muhammad is His prophet." The Islamic faith, which emerged from the Arabian desert in the seventh century C.E., has become one of the world's most important and influential religions.

Within a century after the death of the prophet Muhammad, Islam had spread throughout the Arabian Peninsula into Europe, Africa, and Asia. Today Islam is the world's fastest-growing religion and Muslims can be found throughout the globe. There are about 1.25 billion Muslims, which means that approximately one of every five people follows Islam. The global total of believers has surpassed two older religions, Hinduism and Buddhism; only Christianity has more followers.

Muslims can also be found in North America. Many Muslims have immigrated to the United States and Canada, and large numbers of people—particularly African Americans—have converted to Islam since the 1960s. Today, there are an estimated 6 million Muslims in the United States, with an additional half-million Muslims in Canada.

Despite this growing popularity, many people in the West are uninformed about Islam. For many Americans, their only exposure to this important religion, with its glorious history and rich culture, is through news reports about wars in Muslim countries, terrorist attacks, or fundamentalist denunciations of Western corruption.

The purpose of the INTRODUCING ISLAM series is to provide an objective examination of Islam and give an overview of what Muslims believe, how they practice their faith, and what values they hold most important. Four volumes in particular focus on Islamic beliefs and religious practices. *Islam: The Basics* answers the essential questions about the faith and provides information about the major sects. *Islam, Christianity, and Judaism* describes and explains the similarities and differences between these three great monotheistic religions. *Heroes and Holy Places* gives information about such important figures as Muhammad and Saladin, as well as shrines like Mecca and Jerusalem. *Islamic Fundamentalism* focuses on the emergence of the Islamist movement during the 20th century, the development of an Islamist government in Iran, and the differences between Islamists and moderates in such countries as Algeria, Indonesia, and Egypt.

Two volumes in the series explore Islam in the United States, and the relationship between the Muslim world and the West. *The American Encounter with Islam* provides specific history about Muslims in North America from the 17th century until the present, and traces the development of uniquely American sects like the Nation of Islam. *Muslims and the West* attempts to put the encounter between two important civilizations in broader perspective from a historical point of view.

Recent statistical data is extensively provided in two volumes, in order to discuss life in the Muslim world. *Who Are the Muslims?* is a geopolitical survey that explores the many different cultures that can be found in the Muslim world, as well as the different types of Islamic governments. *What Muslims Think and How They Live* uses information collected in a landmark survey of the Islamic world by the Gallup Organization, as well as other socioeconomic data, to examine Muslim attitudes toward a variety of questions and issues.

As we enter a new century, cultural and political tensions between Muslims and non-Muslims continue. Now more than ever, it is important for people to learn more about their neighbors of all faiths. It is only through education and tolerance that we will be able to build a new world in which fear and mistrust are replaced with brotherhood and peace.

Islam is a global faith, and most Muslims live outside the Middle East. These women are among the more than 205 million Muslims who live in Indonesia.

Tradition and Diversity

A *Muslim* is a follower of *Islam*, one of the world's three great *monotheistic* faiths. The shared religious experience unites Muslims in a worldwide community of believers called the *umma*. However, the questions "Where do Muslims live?" and "How are Muslims governed?" cannot be answered in a simple way. Today Muslims live in practically every country in the world, and they follow a wide variety of cultural practices.

ISLAM AROUND THE WORLD

Although Islam is often identified with the place of its birth, the Arabian Peninsula, today it is a global faith

9

practiced throughout the world by more than 1.25 billion people. The Islamic world stretches from Africa to Indonesia and includes more than 50 countries. Throughout this region there are many cultural differences.

Islam emerged on the Arabian Peninsula during the seventh century, and today in most Arab countries 90 to 95 percent of the people are Muslims. However, some of the largest countries in the area historically known as the Middle East have large non-Arab Muslim populations, such as Turkey (67 million Muslims) and Iran (66 million Muslims).

Asia is actually home to the countries with the largest Muslim populations. Indonesia, for example, is the world's largest Muslim nation; it claims more than 205 million followers of Islam. There are also large Muslim populations in Pakistan (145 million) and India (125 million). In Central Asia, Afghanistan is home to more than 28 million Muslims, who make up 99 percent of the country's population. Numerous other countries in that region have significant Muslim populations; many of these had been part of the Union of Soviet Socialist Republics (U.S.S.R.) until it fragmented in 1991. (The practice of Islam had been prohibited under the strict Communist rule of the Soviet Union.) Today, with nearly 90 percent of its citizens adherents of Islam, the former Soviet republic of Turkmenistan has a Muslim population of about 4.25 million; neighboring Uzbekistan, with a similar proportion of Muslims but a much larger population, has more than 22 million Muslims. Islam is also the majority religion in Azerbaijan and in Kazakhstan (which is 47 percent Muslim and 44 percent Orthodox Christian), while Russia itself has a Muslim population of about 20 million.

Muslim Arabs conquered northern Africa during the seventh and eighth centuries, bringing their religion and culture with them. Islam remains the dominant religion in North African countries from Mauritania to Somalia. The religion spread throughout eastern and sub-Saharan Africa primarily through trade and missionary work. Today, 30 percent of all Africans are

Muslims. Egypt, Nigeria, and Algeria have the continent's largest Muslim populations.

Although Muslims represent only a small percentage of the total population of western Europe, they may be found in fairly large numbers in France, Germany, and the United Kingdom. Each of these European countries controlled colonies in the Islamic world during the 19th and early 20th centuries, and they permitted Muslims to immigrate. Some Muslims went to Europe in search of work, while others sought to escape persecution in their native countries. However, Muslim immigrants were sometimes permitted only as temporary guest workers in the European countries. The greatest difficulty for the Muslim minority has been to fit in with Europe's predominantly Christian and *secular* societies while retaining their own religious identities and Islamic values.

The percentage of Muslims living in South America is small. But there are significant communities of believers in Guyana (about 70,000) and in Suriname (about 85,000).

While the United States does not maintain official statistics on religious affiliation, the U.S. Muslim population is widely estimated at approximately 6 million. Nearly 2 million of the U.S. Muslims are African Americans who have converted to Islam since the 1960s. While Muslims live in every state of the Union, the largest Muslim populations may be found in New York, Michigan, and California.

Meanwhile, Canada is home to about half a million Muslims.

DIVERSITY OF PRACTICES

Muslims believe that their religion transcends nationality and that all Muslims are bound together by their faith. However, while the religious practices of Muslims may be similar, their lifestyles and customs often vary according to where they live; radically different political and cultural settings all but guarantee some differences in the daily lives of Muslims around the world. The most obvious differences among Muslims who live in different countries

Muslims can be found in almost every community in the United States. This Islamic center, for example, is located in Cedar Rapids, Iowa. Today the U.S. Muslim population is estimated at about 6 million.

are the ways in which they dress and their customs regarding events such as marriage and childbirth. For instance, when it comes to daily activities, Bosnian Muslims have more in common with Bosnian Christians than with Muslims who live in Pakistan. In other cases Islamic practices have been influenced by their settings. In Indonesia, for example, aspects of Asian culture have been integrated into Islamic rituals and ceremonies.

In some countries, local traditions show the desire of Muslims to set themselves apart from neighboring non-Muslim cultures. One notable example of this practice occurs in India, where Muslims tend to eat specific foods and to avoid using certain colors and decorations in their wedding ceremonies in order to distinguish themselves from Hindus. In India, Muslims form only 12 percent of the population, and many feel it is important that their religious practices be unique and separate from those of the majority Hindus.

The Islamic world today is highly diverse, with Muslims in different places claiming different ethnic backgrounds and national identities, occupying a range of socioeconomic statuses, speaking different languages, and holding divergent attitudes toward the modern world. The purpose of this book is to provide demographic information about how the worldwide Muslim population is distributed, as well as to give an overview of governments in the Islamic world today. In preparation, earlier chapters provide basic information about the religious beliefs of Muslims, a background about the history of Islamic government, and the basis for Islamic law.

An ornate stained-glass window decorates a mosque, or Muslim place of worship. Islam, one of the world's major monotheistic religions, originated nearly 1,400 years ago with revelations received by the prophet Muhammad.

The Development of Islam

By the beginning of the seventh century C.E., the people living in the area known today as the Middle East practiced a variety of religions, including Judaism, Christianity, and Zoroastrianism. On the Arabian Peninsula, *polytheism*, or belief in multiple gods, predominated. The Arabs worshipped a variety of local deities and idols. One of these deities, called *Allah* (the Arabic name for God), had a greater following than others. Many Arabs prayed to him during times of great distress, though they considered Allah simply one of many gods, albeit with a higher station than the others. Muslims refer to the spiritual position of the Arab world at this time as a state of ignorance, or *al-Jahiliyya*.

During the early part of the seventh century, a new monotheistic religion, Islam, emerged in the Arabian

Peninsula. Within a few short decades, not only had the entire peninsula converted, but adherents had also begun to spread the new faith throughout the region, North Africa, and Central Asia. At the center of this new religion's founding was an Arab merchant and leader named Muhammad Ibn Abd Allah.

MUHAMMAD AND THE BEGINNINGS OF ISLAM

Muhammad was born in the city of Mecca (Makka), which is located in the western part of the Arabian Peninsula, around the

A Muslim prays in Mecca, the birthplace of Muhammad and spiritual center of Islam.

year 570 C.E. When he was about 40 years old, Muhammad began to receive messages from Allah, which were given to him by an angel, Gabriel. The most important message was that Allah is the only God. God also explained to Muhammad how humans should worship Him and live their lives, and He instructed Muhammad to proclaim this message to others. Muhammad soon began to spread God's message, preaching that all people should submit to God's will. The religion became known as Islam, a word derived from the Arabic verb *aslama*, which means "submitted."

Initially, not all of Mecca's citizens were receptive to the message Muhammad proclaimed. Many among the wealthy regarded Islam as a threat to their power and position; many other Arabs refused to give up their worship of pagan idols. Mecca's leaders persecuted Muhammad and his followers, and in 622 the Prophet and a group of Muslims left Mecca for the city of Yathrib (which was later renamed Madina, or "City of the Prophet"). This journey, known as the ***hijra***, was an important milestone in the history of Islam and marks the beginning of the Islamic calendar. In Yathrib, Muhammad was able to preach freely as the spiritual and political leader of a growing Muslim community. Many people of Yathrib joined Islam, and the first Islamic government was established.

War between the Meccans and the Muslims continued sporadically over the next few years, until the two sides signed a peace treaty in 628. The next year, however, the Meccans breached the treaty. In January 630 Muhammad led an army to Mecca, whose dispirited residents surrendered without a fight. After this, many Meccans converted to Islam, as did the members of various Arab tribes in the region. By the time the Prophet died in 632, Muslims controlled the areas around Mecca and Madina.

ISLAM, JUDAISM, AND CHRISTIANITY

Muslims believe Muhammad was the last in a line of prophets to whom God had given divine messages. Previous prophets included

Abraham, Moses, and Jesus—major figures in the development of Judaism and Christianity. All three of the world's major monotheistic faiths trace their origins to the patriarch Abraham—Judaism and Christianity through Abraham's younger son, Isaac, and Islam through his older son, Ishmael. Muslims also consider Allah to be the same God worshipped by Jews and Christians.

Despite these similarities, there are fundamental differences between Islam, Judaism, and Christianity. Muslims consider the commandments of the Jewish Torah, traditionally ascribed to Moses, and Jesus' teachings as recorded in the Christian Gospels to be divinely inspired, but they believe the original messages from God became distorted over time. For example, Muslims believe that although Jesus relayed God's divine message, Christians later distorted the Scriptures by inserting into them the claim that Jesus was the Son of God. Thus Muslims consider it Islam's primary mission to proclaim God's uncorrupted message and replace the older Jewish and Christian traditions with the newer and more authentic Islamic ones. While they respect both the Torah and the Bible, they consider the *Qur'an*—the messages received by Muhammad—as the final, and most important, of God's messages to humanity.

THE CALIPHS

When Muhammad died in 632, he had no son who could take over his position as leader of the Muslims. Muhammad had not publicly named a successor, and the Qur'an offered no specific guidance for choosing one. A group of the Prophet's close companions in Madina selected his trustworthy companion and father-in-law, Abu Bakr, to be the *caliph* (successor), or the political and religious leader of the Muslims. As the first caliph, Abu Bakr took over the worldly authority of the Prophet. While most Muslims accepted Abu Bakr as the legitimate leader, some had supported the claim to succession of Muhammad's cousin and son-in-law, Ali.

A seminal event in the history of Islam was the *hijra*, or migration from Mecca to Yathrib (Madina), in C.E. 622. The building above is the Prophet's Mosque in Madina, where Muslims believe Muhammad was buried after his death in 632.

The decision to choose a single successor to Muhammad to lead the Muslims had a great impact on the development of Islam. "In sudden crisis, a decision of world-shaking significance had been reached," explains John Alden Williams, an expert on Islamic civilization, in his book *Islam*. "Had each tribe elected its own leaders, the unity Muhammad imposed on the quarrelsome Arabs would soon have been dissipated. Had the Muslims decided to be governed by a council of the leading Companions, Islamic government would have developed along oligarchic or republican lines; instead, it has historically tended to be characterized by one-man rule."

Once the caliph was chosen, it became necessary to enforce his rule, because some of the Arab tribes refused to obey. During Abu Bakr's two years as caliph, the Muslims forced tribes that had not accepted the caliph to recognize his authority. In addition, tribes in other parts of the Arabian Peninsula, which had not previously been under the authority of Islam, were brought under the caliph's control.

After Abu Bakr died in 634, Umar became the second caliph. Under his rule, Muslim armies conquered Iraq, Egypt, Syria, and Palestine. These conquests of areas that had been controlled by two larger empires—the Byzantine Empire, centered in modern-day Turkey, and the Persian Empire, based in present-day Iran—happened very quickly, and they changed the nature of the Islamic community. All of a sudden, the Islamic world encompassed the traditions and languages of a greater variety of cultures and countries, just as it does today. Umar ruled for 10 years, successfully managing the expanding Islamic empire, before being assassinated in 644. After his death, the Muslim community went through a period of dissension and rivalry. No caliph who came after Umar enjoyed the widespread Muslim support he had commanded.

Before he died, Umar appointed a committee of his peers to choose his successor. The committee first asked Ali, Muhammad's son-in-law and cousin, to become caliph. However, the committee required that Ali accept certain rulings made by his predecessors. This Ali refused to do, as he felt that the first two caliphs had strayed from Muhammad's original views and intentions. As a result, the committee selected Uthman, another of Muhammad's sons-in-law, as the third caliph.

Uthman was not nearly as strong a leader as Umar had been, and during the time he ruled (644–656) he did little to expand Muslim power. He was criticized because he gave members of his family powerful positions and large amounts of land in the conquered provinces. This caused discontent among the Muslims, as most believed that the fruits of the conquest should be shared equally among all the members of the Muslim community.

Perhaps Uthman's most important accomplishment was creating an official text of the Qur'an. Prior to his rule, the Qur'an existed in various written and unwritten forms. Muhammad had originally recited the messages of God to his followers, who had memorized the verses. Some messages had been written down on pieces of bone or scraps of paper; others were handed down through memory. Muhammad himself could not read or write, so he never created an authoritative scripture. As a result, by 644 there were many variant texts, and some included false verses. Uthman oversaw the collection of these texts and their careful review by Muhammad's surviving companions, as well as scholars and religious leaders. Verses judged to differ from the exact words God had originally revealed through Muhammad, and verses believed to have been created in the years after the Prophet's death, were destroyed. The "true" verses were then organized together into the Qur'an. In doing this, Uthman prevented the spread of textual variations that might have splintered the faith.

In 656 Uthman was killed by Egyptian rebels who attacked his house in Madina. After his death, Ali was again asked to become caliph. At first, he refused the position because Uthman had been murdered, but he consented after delegations of Muslims from Madina and other provinces urged him to accept.

UNREST DURING ALI'S RULE

Ali was one of the closest living relatives of Muhammad, and he had been one of the Prophet's earliest followers. Ali believed that he understood exactly what God had envisioned for Islam and for the Muslim community. Some Muslims agreed, and these supporters of Ali considered him the only legitimate leader of the Muslims after Muhammad's death. However, Ali did not have universal support in the Muslim community. After he became caliph several influential leaders opposed his rule, including Muhammad's widow, Aisha, and Uthman's cousin Muawiya, governor of the Islamic province of Syria.

Because Ali did not enjoy the same support as the three previous caliphs, he moved from Madina to Kufa, a city in present-day Iraq where many of his supporters lived, and made it the new capital of the Islamic state. Aisha and her supporters then moved to Basra (also in present-day Iraq). In 656 Ali's and Aisha's supporters fought the Battle of the Camel (so named because the fighting swirled around Aisha's camel, from which she observed the battle). This was the first major conflict that

Shiite Muslims in Pakistan celebrate Ashura, which commemorates the martyrdom of Ali's son Hussein at the Battle of Karbala in 680. Today, Shiites make up about 14 percent of the total Muslim population.

involved Muslims fighting against Muslims. Ali's troops emerged victorious, but the battle represented a breach of the brotherhood preached by Islam.

Ali's next battle was against Muawiya, who challenged him for the caliphate on the grounds that Ali had not done enough to capture Uthman's assassins. He demanded that Ali deliver the assassins if he did not wish to be considered an accomplice in Uthman's murder. In 657 the soldiers of Ali and Muawiya fought at Siffin, located on the Euphrates River in northern Syria. At one point during the battle, soldiers in Muawiya's army placed pages from the Qur'an on the tips of their spears, and Ali's troops refused to fight against them.

Muawiya then asked for arbitrators to settle the dispute. Ali agreed, but this proved to be a mistake on his part. During the arbitration, Muawiya's representative outmaneuvered Ali's negotiator. Worse, some of Ali's followers were angry that he had submitted to arbitration, and they turned against him. This group became known as the Kharijites, or "seceders." Although Ali continued to serve as caliph, his authority had been undermined, and he lost the support he had once enjoyed.

The Kharijites became a problem for Ali because they believed that he had no right to agree to arbitration to resolve the disagreement. They accused him of disobeying a verse in the Qur'an that reads, "If one party rebels against the other, fight against that which rebels" (Qur'an 49:9). Ali and his troops fought the Kharijites in 658 at Nahrawan in central Iraq. Although his troops finally won the battle, many Muslims were killed in the process, which caused Ali to lose even more support in the Muslim community. In 661 a Kharijite assassin murdered Ali. After his death, Ali's son Hassan agreed not to contend for the caliphate, and Muawiya took power.

Abu Bakr, Umar, Uthman, and Ali, the first four caliphs, are known as the al-Khulafa' al-Rashidun (the rightly guided caliphs). They had all known Muhammad personally and had worked directly with him to build the Islamic community. Their approximately 30 years of rule (from 632 to 661) were marked by great accomplishments and the remarkable spread of Islam.

It is important to mention that the Battle of Siffin was the cause of the division of the Muslim community into two major *sects*, Sunnis and Shiites, and a minor one, Kharijites (later called Ibadis). The name *Sunni* comes from an Arabic word meaning "the path," because these Muslims follow the path they believe Muhammad intended. Today, the Sunnis are the largest group of Muslims worldwide, making up about 85 percent of the global Muslim community. Sunni Muslims generally believe that religious leadership should not be in the hands of ruling political authorities, but instead belongs to the Muslim community at large. They also believe that, while religious figures may exercise significant political or social power, committees of believers in each community should be responsible for the management of the community's *mosque* and land.

There are differing views over the emergence of the Shiite sect. Some believe, for example. the sect began to form as soon as Muhammad passed away. The commonly accepted view, however, is that the followers of Ali did not become known as Shiites until after the Battle of Siffin. The word "Shiite" is from the Arabic term *shia*, meaning "followers" or "party." Though the word refers to the followers or party of anybody, such as the Shia of Muawiya, in time, the term came to be used only in reference to Ali's followers. The Shiites, the followers of Ali and later of his sons Hassan and Hussein, developed a religious doctrine based on the authority and sinlessness of Ali and his descendants, referred to as *imams*. According to Shiite traditions, the Imam was both a spiritual and an earthly leader, and each Imam after Ali had to be a direct descendant of Ali. Furthermore, Shiite teaching held that the Imam was incapable of committing sin or error and that he was omnipresent in the world as an abiding source of divine guidance. The difference in political theory between Shiites and Sunnis would lead to tension in the years to come.

The magnificent Dome of the Rock in Jerusalem is one of the first important works of Islamic architecture. It was commissioned by the Umayyad caliph Abd al-Malik, and completed in 691. Muslims believe the shrine was built over a rock on which Muhammad stood during his "night journey" from Mecca to Jerusalem, which is described in the Qur'an (Sura 17). The Al-Aqsa Mosque is located nearby.

THE UMAYYADS

Muawiya was the first of the Umayyad caliphs, a dynasty that ruled the Islamic world from 661 until 750. In 661 he moved the capital of the Islamic state to the city of Damascus, in Syria, where he was already governor. He also made the caliphate hereditary, meaning that the title passed from relative to relative, normally from father to son.

Under the Umayyad dynasty, the Islamic state became an imperial power, as military expeditions greatly expanded the empire. The Muslims conquered territories in Afghanistan, Central Asia, North Africa, and the Iberian Peninsula. Their primary source of military power was an Arab army based in Syria whose soldiers swore personal loyalty to the caliph and served as his personal bodyguards. Although the Muslims were successful in conquering many lands during the time of the Umayyad dynasty, most of the people within the newly expanded empire were not Muslims or Arabs. Instead, they were Christians, Jews, Hindus, Zoroastrians, and pagans. Because the Qur'an encourages tolerance and because Muhammad showed mercy toward the Meccans after his troops conquered them, the Muslims were relatively tolerant rulers. This approach won many converts among conquered peoples.

After Muawiya died in 680, he was succeeded by his son Yazid, whose reign as caliph was marred by corruption and misrule. The Muslim community of Madina refused to recognize Yazid's authority, and Ali's son Hussein also revolted against him. Hussein traveled to Kufa in an attempt to gather support for his revolt, but he found no help among the people there. At Karbala, in southern Iraq, the Umayyads massacred Hussein and a small band of his Shiite followers. Shiites were shocked at this display of violence toward a member of Muhammad's family, as it seemed to contradict everything Muhammad taught and represented.

The revolt of Hussein was one of many faced by the Umayyads during their rule. Kharijites, Shiites, and other dissidents rebelled against the dynasty in the name of Islam and promoted a return to the Islam that had been practiced by Muhammad and his companions. In 750 the Umayyads were toppled from power, and descendants of Muhammad's uncle Abbas seized power. They established the Abbasid dynasty, which lasted from 750 to 1258, and which would hold great power over the Muslim community for the next five centuries. The Shiites remained in opposition, but the Muslim community continued to break into smaller sects.

The events that occurred during the rule of the rightly guided caliphs and the Umayyads shaped the destiny of Islam thereafter.

In the eighth and ninth centuries, the Muslim civilization in southern Spain was the most enlightened in Europe at a time when the continent was suffering through its "Dark Ages." This is the Court of the Lions at Alhambra, a palace in Granada built by the Moors.

The Spread of Islam

By the middle of the eighth century, many important and far-reaching changes in Muslim society had occurred. As a result of Muslim conquests and large-scale conversions to Islam, non-Arab Muslims outnumbered Arab Muslims in many places for the first time. And among non-Arab Muslims, there was widespread discontent over their treatment by Arab Muslims.

Many of the Kharijite or Shiite dissidents who participated in revolts against the Umayyads were non-Arabs who had converted to Islam as it spread into their home areas. For example, in North Africa many of the Kharijites were Berbers who had lived in the region long before the Arabs invaded in the seventh century, and they were upset about discriminatory treatment. Throughout the Islamic world newly converted Muslims demanded equality with the Arab Muslims. They wanted a society in which the promises of Islam were fulfilled—every Muslim could enjoy the same rights and privileges and be subject to the same taxes regardless of ethnicity or background.

In 747 the Abbasid family, members of which were descended from Muhammad's uncle Abbas, organized a revolt among Arab Muslims in Iraq. One of the leaders of the revolt, Abu al-Abbas, claimed the caliphate even before the Abbasid troops had beaten the Umayyad forces. But in 750, after three years of fighting, the Abbasid armies

Muslim scholars preserved ancient works by the Greeks and Romans, translating them into Arabic; they also made great strides in science, medicine, mathematics, and literature. The pages shown here are from an ancient mathematics text (opposite) and a colorfully illustrated storybook (above).

gained a decisive victory when they wiped out an Umayyad army of 12,000 men and forced the Umayyad caliph to flee to Egypt.

From 750 to the mid-800s, the Abbasids altered the Islamic state into an empire that was ruled by an absolute monarch, a system of government different from the one Muhammad had practiced during his lifetime. The new capital of the Abbasids was at Baghdad, a city built by the Abbasid caliph Abu Jafar al-Mansur in 762. This city came to be known by many names, including Madinat al-Salam (the city of peace). As capital of an Islamic empire that during its Golden Age stretched from the Atlantic coast of Africa to the Pacific shores of southern Asia, Baghdad because a thriving metropolis. The Muslims built a huge administrative complex in the middle of Baghdad, and the city's population grew to more than a million.

The Abbasids established an efficient centralized government, and the Muslim empire thrived as a result of its highly productive economic system. Importing and exporting became big businesses, and products from eastern Africa, Arabia, India, Southeast Asia, and China made their way from the Persian Gulf to Baghdad. In addition, goods from North Africa, Egypt, and the Mediterranean were also popular in Baghdad. The early years of the Abbasid dynasty are remembered as a time of a near-ideal Islamic state, with a powerful military, great wealth, and remarkable cultural and scientific growth.

During the time of the Abbasids, Islamic arts and sciences flourished. Under the caliphs Harun al-Rashid (who ruled from 786 to 809) and his son al-Ma'mun (who ruled from 813 to 833), the Muslim Arabs, who had once been unschooled and nomadic, began investigating and learning the scientific and philosophical teachings of the Greeks, Hindus, Persians, and Chinese. In 830 al-Ma'mun created a research library named the House of Wisdom in which educated Christians and Muslims translated the works of Plato, Aristotle, and other Greek philosophers into Arabic. These translations inspired Muslims to develop their own Islamic philosophical tradition, which in turn eventually helped to introduce to the peoples of western Europe many important works and ideas from Greek philosophy that had been forgotten or destroyed after the collapse of the Roman empire in the fifth century. Muslim scientists and mathematicians developed algebra, algorithms, experimental medicine, hospitals, and universities. During this period, scholars developed important schools of Islamic law, and Sufism, the mystical movement in Islam, gained followers.

Despite the many accomplishments of the Abbasids, their caliphs had some worldly weaknesses. They expected to be treated in much the same way as rulers in other parts of the world. They and their families lived in royal fashion and surrounded themselves with thousands of slaves and officials of the state. Where Muhammad had been available to even the lowliest members of the Muslim community, only the most privileged people were permitted to meet with the caliphs. Corrupted by wealth and extravagance, the caliphs neglected their duties as religious leaders.

Another problem was that the authority of the Abbasid caliphs was never completely established in some Islamic territories. For example, after the fall of the Umayyads, a prince of the dynasty named Abd al-Rahman escaped to Spain, where in 756 he founded an Islamic state that lasted until 1031. During the 780s a descendant of Ali's son Hassan, Idris Ibn Abdallah, created an independent kingdom in Morocco. Another revolt from Abbasid hegemony occurred in the 800s when the governors of Tunisia and Egypt broke away from the official Islamic state and formed their own independent states under the Fatimid dynasty. Other rivals to Abbasid rule began to emerge in Turkey and Oman.

The Abbasids' greatest control over the Islamic world was between 750 and 929. After this point, various leaders in different parts of the world claimed to be the legitimate caliph, or ruler of the Muslims. From 929 until 1258, when the Mongol conquest of Baghdad eliminated the last vestiges of Abbasid power, most of the Abbasid caliphs were puppet rulers supported by military leaders.

ISLAM SPREADS EAST

Although Arab armies were largely responsible for spreading Islam in North Africa and the region that today is known as the Middle East, for the most part the religion spread into Asia and eastern Africa by more peaceful means. Muslim traders from Arabia and India were the first people to bring the teachings of Islam to Indonesia. However, the religion's primary influence on the country came later from a port city called Malacca (Melaka),

The Mongols' destruction of Baghdad in 1258, as depicted in a Persian manuscript, marked the end of the caliphate of the Arab Abbasids. However, Islam continued to flourish and spread.

located on the southwestern coast of the Malay Peninsula. During the early 15th century, Malacca gained control of the important trading route that ran through the Strait of Malacca, which was positioned between Malaya and Sumatra. It attracted more than 15,000 merchants from all parts of Asia, including Chinese, Arabs, and Indians, and became a great economic center. Malacca's ruler at the time, a Sumatran prince named Paramesvara (who later changed his own name to Sultan Iskandar Shah), converted to Islam in 1414, and the religion then became very popular in various parts of Indonesia.

As in Indonesia, Islam was introduced to China by Muslim merchants who transported goods such as wool, linen, ivory, and amber to Chang'an, which was then the Chinese capital. The route that these merchants traveled to get to Chang'an eventually became known as the Silk Road. All of the merchants, soldiers, scholars, and craftsmen who moved from the Middle East to China, bringing the tenets of Islam with them, became known as the Hui people (also called the Tonggan). The first Chinese mosque was built in Chang'an in 742.

During the 12th and 13th centuries, the Mongols—led by Genghis Khan and his descendants—moved west into the Islamic lands. Genghis Khan's grandson Hulagu Khan laid siege to Baghdad, and in 1258 the Mongols destroyed the city and killed the last Abbasid caliph. This episode had a lasting effect on the Arab supremacy in Islam: the center of power in the Islamic world shifted away from the Arab world, and it would not return again until the 20th century.

Despite this turmoil, the vitality of Islam did not decrease. Socially and culturally, the Muslim community became more diverse than ever before. By 1313 the Mongols had officially converted to Islam, and the religion continued to spread throughout the 14th century. In Malaysia and on the islands that now make up Indonesia, Muslim merchants and scholars introduced Islam to the local cultures. Eventually, they were successful in converting the rulers of these regions, who then made Islam the official religion of their states. The Muslim population also grew in

Islam spread into Asia and East Africa primarily through trade and missionary work. Arab sailors like the ones manning the *dhow* in the 12th-century
book illustration pictured above had introduced Islam throughout the
Indian Ocean by the 9th century. (Opposite, bottom) The detail from a
14th-century map shows a caravan following the Silk Road, a network of
trade routes between the eastern Mediterranean Sea and China; the body
of water to the left represents the Caspian Sea.

China thanks to the influence of Muslim merchants. In the eastern part of sub-Saharan Africa, many people converted to Islam during the 1400s; most of these conversions were the result of trade and personal contact rather than military action.

CONFLICTS WITH THE WEST

While Islam expanded into Asia through generally peaceful means, the encounter between Muslims and the West was marked by greater violence. When the Arab Muslims spread into North Africa in the seventh and eighth centuries, they had taken over territories controlled by the Byzantine Empire. The Byzantine Empire was the eastern half of the once-mighty Roman Empire; based in the city of Constantinople (modern-day Istanbul, Turkey), it had survived the fall of Rome to Germanic tribes in the fifth century. The Byzantine Empire had long been engaged in wars with the Persian Empire to the east. The spread of Islam into Persia, as well as into Byzantine territories in Africa and the Middle East, made fighting between Muslim and Byzantine armies almost certain. By the 11th century, the Muslims had captured a great deal of territory formerly controlled by the Byzantines, and they were threatening Constantinople itself.

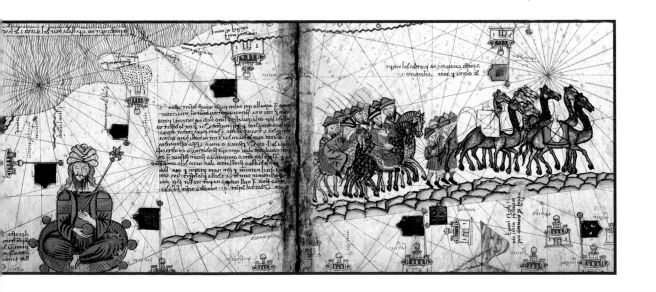

At the same time, Islam had spread into western Europe. Arab-Berber Moors had invaded the Iberian Peninsula as early as 711, establishing Muslim centers of learning in the region in southern Spain called Andalusia. The Muslims in Spain soon built a civilization in which trade and agriculture flourished, and in which Muslims, Christians, and Jews lived together in relative peace. Spanish Muslims made valuable contributions to science and the arts. Soon Córdoba was the most sophisticated city in Europe. According to 10th-century writings, Córdoba had a population more than 10 times greater than Paris, and it was home to 700 mosques and more than 70 libraries, one of which reportedly had a collection exceeding 500,000 manuscripts.

For centuries Córdoba, in southern Spain, was the center of Islamic civilization in Europe. The Torre de la Calahorra (tower of Calahorra) in Córdoba dates to 1369; today it houses the Museum of the Three Cultures (Muslim, Christian, and Jewish).

But other Europeans continued to fight with the Muslims in their midst. By the 11th century, Christians under Alfonso VI (ca. 1030–1109), king of León and Castile, had made advances into Muslim territory, and in 1085 Alfonso's forces captured the city of Toledo. This marked the beginning of four centuries of fighting to expel Muslims from the Iberian Peninsula, a period later called the *Reconquista*, or reconquest, by the Christians. In 1492 the Reconquista was completed when the armies of King Ferdinand and Queen Isabella captured Granada, the last Muslim stronghold on the peninsula. After this, the rulers expelled all Muslims and Jews from their kingdoms, which were united into modern Spain.

THE CRUSADES

At nearly the same time that the Reconquista was beginning on the Iberian Peninsula, Christian knights from other parts of Europe were turning toward the Muslim lands to the east. Worried that Constantinople might fall to encroaching Turkish armies, the Byzantine emperor Alexius I Comnenus appealed to Pope Urban II, head of the powerful Roman Catholic Church, for help. On November 27, 1095, Pope Urban spoke in a field in Clermont, France, and called on Christians to fight a holy war, or crusade, against the Muslims. The pope urged European Christians to travel east and help the Byzantine Christians eliminate the Turkish threat from their borders, then capture Jerusalem and other Christian holy places the Muslims had controlled since the eighth century. As an incentive, the pope promised that Christians who died in battle would have their sins immediately forgiven. People all across Europe willingly responded to the pope's message.

The First Crusade was launched in 1096, in two waves. The first wave, known as the "Peasants' Crusade" because it was made up of common people and poorer knights, was under-equipped and unprepared. Most of these crusaders were slaughtered when they reached Turkey, at the Battle of Civetot. A second group of crusaders, which

This detail from an illuminated manuscript shows English and French knights sailing to the Holy Land. The Crusades, a series of wars conducted between 1095 and 1291, pitted invading Christian Europeans against the Muslims of Turkey and the eastern Mediterranean.

included the more experienced and better-equipped knights of Europe, began their journey east in the fall of 1096. When these crusaders arrived at Constantinople, they rested and gathered fresh supplies. In the spring of 1097 the crusaders set out to battle Turkish armies. After capturing Nicaea, capital of the Seljuk Turks, the crusaders embarked on a long and difficult campaign down the Mediterranean coast, eventually reaching Jerusalem. When the

Christian armies finally broke into the walled city in June 1099, they massacred the Muslims and Jews living there. After sacking Jerusalem, some of the crusaders returned to Europe. Those who remained established four small Christian kingdoms along the Mediterranean coast: Jerusalem, Edessa, Antioch, and Tripoli. They built castles from which they could defend these kingdoms.

The four Crusader Kingdoms were never completely at peace with their Muslim neighbors. They were small Christian states surrounded by the Muslims whose land they had taken. Relations between the two groups were complex. To secure their borders, the crusaders frequently raided and skirmished with the Muslims. They sometimes mistreated Muslims living within their kingdoms. Nonetheless, the Christian settlers also traded with Muslims and intermarried with them.

In 1144 Muslim forces under the command of Imad al-Din Zangi conquered Edessa, in northern Syria. In response to this news, a Roman Catholic priest named Bernard of Clairvaux traveled throughout France and Germany in 1146, calling for another crusade. This motivated tens of thousands of people to leave their homes and embark on the Second Crusade.

The political aims of the First Crusade had been to help the Byzantine Empire secure its borders and to capture Jerusalem and other Christian holy places. The political aims of the Second Crusade were to force the Muslims out of Jerusalem completely, to strengthen the Crusader Kingdoms, and to assist the Reconquista by removing Muslims from Spain. There was another purpose as well: the Christian Church had split into eastern (Orthodox) and western (Roman Catholic) branches, and a goal of the crusaders was to spread Roman Catholicism into eastern Europe.

King Louis of France and King Conrad of Germany led the armies of the Second Crusade. When the travelers entered the Byzantine Empire, Louis maintained discipline among his troops. He did not allow them to abuse the townspeople and farmers. Unfortunately, Conrad did not maintain such order, and his troops robbed and mistreated the Orthodox Christians. Their disrespect for the Byzantine citizens further strained the relations between eastern and western Europeans.

Before the crusaders reached the Middle East, King Conrad grew ill and had to return to Europe. This left King Louis in charge of the crusader army. Though devoutly religious, Louis was not a military leader, and the Muslims easily defeated the crusaders. When the Christian knights returned to Europe, the Crusader Kingdoms were more vulnerable than they had been before.

Within a few decades the Muslims, under the leadership of the great Kurdish general Saladin, began to recapture cities from the Christians, including Jerusalem in 1187. In response, Pope Gregory VIII called for a Third Crusade. The response was less enthusiastic this time, and the armies of the Third Crusade did not sail for the Middle East until 1190. One reason for the slow response was that France and England were fighting each other. The Third Crusade could not begin until England's King Richard I and France's King Philip II reached a truce. After the two countries settled their differences, their armies sailed to the Holy Land. A powerful army from Germany, which was ruled by Emperor Frederick I, also set out on the Third Crusade, but after Frederick died during the journey most of his army returned home.

After a long siege, the crusaders captured Acre (Akka), a city on the Mediterranean coast, in 1191. Afterward, King Richard ordered the massacre of nearly 3,000 Muslim prisoners on a hill outside the city. Although the English king is popularly known in the West as Richard the Lion-Hearted, Muslims remember him for this brutal act as the "Butcher of Ayyadieh."

After capturing Acre, Richard and his army continued marching along the coast toward Jerusalem. He won an important victory at Jaffa in 1192, but his army was not strong enough to capture Jerusalem. Instead, the Christian and Muslim armies became locked in a stalemate. After several months, Richard and Saladin

The ancient city of Jerusalem is considered holy by the followers of the three major monotheistic faiths: Judaism, Christianity, and Islam. Because of Jerusalem's special status, Christians and Muslims often fought for control of the city during the Crusades.

negotiated a five-year truce that stabilized the borders between the Christians and Muslims. The Muslims would retain control of Jerusalem, but unarmed Christian pilgrims would be permitted to visit the holy city without fear of being attacked. The crusaders would also keep control of Acre and the coastal territory they had captured. This provided some peace and stability for the weak Crusader Kingdoms.

Over the next 100 years, numerous other crusades were mounted, but none proved particularly successful. Soldiers of the Fourth Crusade, which embarked in 1199, ended up sacking Constantinople, the city they had vowed to protect, and never fought any Muslim armies at all. By 1291 the Muslims had launched a final offensive to drive out the Europeans and destroy the Crusader Kingdoms.

The Taj Mahal at Agra, India, built during the mid-17th century, is an exquisite example of Islamic architecture. The Mughal emperor Shah Jahan commissioned the structure in memory of his wife, who had died in childbirth.

THE RISE OF MUSLIM EMPIRES

By the 16th century, three powerful empires controlled most of the Islamic world. These were the Ottoman Empire, based in present-day Turkey; the Safavid dynasty in Iran; and the Mughal Empire in India.

The Ottoman Empire was the longest lived of these three powerful empires, lasting until shortly after World War I. The Ottoman Turks who ruled the empire took their name from Osman I, a Turkish chieftain who had founded an Islamic state in Anatolia in the late 1200s. The Ottomans gradually expanded their power and influence at the expense of the Christian Byzantine Empire. Finally, in 1453, they conquered Constantinople, the Byzantine capital. The Ottoman Turks made the city the center of their dominion and later renamed it Istanbul.

During the 1500s, under the reign of Süleyman the Magnificent, the Muslim community achieved its greatest level of accord since the early reign of the Abbasids. The Ottomans proclaimed themselves "defenders and protectors of Islam," and in this capacity they justified their conquest of Islamic territories. They spread their control into North Africa, Central Asia, the Arabian Peninsula, and even eastern Europe. However, under Ottoman rule people of distinct cultures retained their individual identities within the Muslim society. Although the Ottoman sultans were Turkish, many of the officials and military personnel in their service hailed from countries throughout the Mediterranean region. Furthermore, large numbers of the Ottoman aristocrats were skilled in the arts, languages, and literature, which helped to set the cultural standards for all Muslims.

The Ottomans' primary rivals were the Safavids, a ruling dynasty that came to power in Persia (modern-day Iran) around 1501 under Ismail I. By 1512 the Safavids ruled most of Persia and Mesopotamia (modern-day Iraq). It was during the Safavid era that most of the people of Persia converted to Shiism, and today Shiites continue to constitute a majority in Iran as well as in Iraq.

Despite their shared Islamic beliefs, the Ottomans and the Safavids fought a series of devastating wars through the middle of the 17th century. The fighting, though inconclusive, drained both empires of their resources. After a period of decline, the Safavid Empire was finally eliminated in the 1730s.

A Central Asian prince named Babur founded the Mughal Empire of India in 1526. Babur's troops were able to defeat armies much larger than theirs using firearms. The Mughal Empire reached its highest point under a ruler named Akbar, who reigned from 1556 to 1605. Under his rule, the Mughal Empire covered two-thirds of South Asia, including most of present-day Afghanistan, Pakistan, north and central India, and Bangladesh. Akbar was a successful leader at least in part because of his tolerance of a variety of religious beliefs. Over time, however, this tolerant attitude was abandoned, and the empire suffered a long decline before its last vestiges were swept away by 1858.

COLONIALISM AND THE MUSLIM RESPONSE

A major reason for the downfall of each of these powerful Muslim empires was the growing involvement of European countries in the Islamic world. For example, Great Britain became involved in India during the 18th century, and in 1765 the Mughal emperor permitted the British East India Company, a trading organization closely linked to the British government, to rule over parts of the country. By 1858 the British controlled the entire country as part of their vast colonial empire. Britain had also been involved in Persia during the 17th century, sending military technology to keep the Safavid shahs (kings) in power in exchange for trade considerations.

Other European countries were also involved in the Islamic world. Among the first were the Portuguese, who had captured cities on the east coast of Africa and throughout the Indian

Ocean to use as trading posts for their ships in the 16th century. The French dealt a surprising blow to the Islamic world when an army commanded by Napoleon invaded Egypt in 1798. The quick surrender of this territory by the Mamluks, who ruled Egypt in the name of the Ottoman sultan, surprised many Muslims. Russian and Austrian armies also captured Ottoman territory during the 18th century. The main reason for the success of the West was its technological advances, such as the development of firearms and cannons, which gave military superiority to European forces.

During the 19th century, European countries established colonies throughout the Islamic world. Great Britain, for example, ruled over parts of sub-Saharan Africa, Egypt and the Sudan, many Caribbean islands, India, and other parts of Asia. The British had a great deal of influence in Persia and in the small Arab kingdoms located along the coast of the Red Sea (these became known as the Trucial States because of their agreements with the British). Other European countries, such as France, Germany, and Italy, also held colonies in Africa or Asia.

Colonialism sparked dramatic changes within all Muslim communities. In addition to enacting a great number of administrative changes in governance, colonial authorities removed Islam from its former central role in social and economic organization. Most important, perhaps, the colonial governments reorganized Islamic law and blended it with their own European legal systems. To this day, most Islamic countries have a dual legal system as a result of colonialism. The laws governing most personal matters are based on Islamic law, but most criminal and trade laws are based on European legal models.

During the colonial period, several Muslim reform movements came into being, the most influential of which was the *Salafiyya* (Way of the Ancestors). Jamal al-Din al-Afghani (d. 1897), a politician and philosopher whose birthplace and citizenship are a matter of controversy (some assert that he was an Iranian, and others that he was an Afghani), and Muhammad Abdu (d. 1905), an

Egyptian theologian and expert on Islamic law, were early supporters of this movement. The goal of Salafiyya was to reform Islam using modern Western notions of science and reasoning. In addition, Afghani helped to start the Pan-Islamism movement, which called for the unity of all Muslims throughout the world, a goal he feared might be threatened by nationalism. Muhammad Abdu's primary concerns were *theology* and reform of Islamic law, as he rejected the unquestioned acceptance of historical events and philosophy.

The most significant successors of the Salafiyya movement were the Muslim Brotherhood, the Jamaat-i-Islami, and the Muhammadiya. Hasan al-Banna (d. 1949), a teacher in Egypt, started the Muslim Brotherhood in 1928. This Muslim organization helped to inspire Islamic reform movements in several other Arab countries, including Jordan, Syria, and Sudan. Although the Muslim Brotherhood began as a religious and charitable organization that promoted morality and charitable works, it evolved into a more political organization, and its members called for the replacement of secular governments with governments based on Islamic doctrine. Today the Muslim Brotherhood continues to exert considerable influence on the international Muslim community, and it is associated with Islamic reform movements in such non-Arab countries as Pakistan, Bangladesh, and Malaysia. Its reach also extends into Islamic communities in the United States.

Abu al-Ala Mawdudi (d. 1979), who was dedicated to the cause of reviving Islam in India, started the Jamaat-i-Islami in 1941. When British rule ended in India in 1947, he called for the creation of an Islamic republic in Pakistan. The Jamaat-i-Islami has supported conservative Muslim politics since its inception. Its leaders have favored limiting the influence of minority Islamic sects in Pakistan, and they have also stirred up opposition to secular governments. Even though its political influence declined after the death of Abu al-Ala Mawdudi in 1979, the Jamaat-i-Islami continues to attract the loyalty of university students and of lower-middle-class citizens. It is also still quite influential among Pakistani immigrants to both Europe and the United States.

The Muhammadiya is the largest Muslim reform society in Southeast Asia. Its founders started it on Java, an Indonesian island, in 1912, and its values were heavily influenced by the opinions and beliefs of Muhammad Abdu. The Muhammadiya supports an Islam based on reason, and, most notably, it has called for the social liberation and equality of Muslim women. The Muhammadiya's women's organization, Aishiya, is named for the prophet Muhammad's wife, and it is one of the most active and productive women's organizations in the international Muslim community.

An Asian man performs one of the daily prayers required by Islam. No matter where they live, all Muslims are united by the required practices of their religion, known as the Five Pillars.

What Muslims Believe

Despite the wide variety of people who follow Islam, all committed Muslims share certain beliefs and practices. The most important obligations of the religion, performed by all Muslims, are known as the five pillars of Islam. The religion's fundamental requirements and restrictions are primarily based on teachings found in the Qur'an, the holy book of Islam, in which God's messages to humanity, as revealed to the prophet Muhammad, were recorded. After the Qur'an, the most important Islamic text is the *Hadith*, a collection of the sayings and actions of Muhammad and his closest followers (known as the Companions).

THE QUR'AN, ISLAM'S HOLY SCRIPTURE

Although the Qur'an includes the messages from God that Muhammad shared with his followers, it was not compiled as a text until a few years after the Prophet's death. Muhammad himself could not read or write, and during his lifetime, the Companions were more likely to memorize his teachings than to write them down. As a result, the Prophet's teachings were recorded in many different ways.

After Muhammad's death, followers of Islam began to argue about what the Prophet had actually said. Therefore, it became an important goal of Muslims to create a definitive text of God's revelations to Muhammad so as to avoid confusion and dispute. A committee of Companions collected verses that had been recorded over the years and compiled the text that became the Qur'an. The book was completed by Muhammad's third successor, Uthman Ibn Affan, who had ordered the compilation of the verses to ensure their preservation, as the Companions were gradually dying. In order to create the authoritative text, Uthman collected all of the written parchments of the Qur'an and compared them with what the Companions had memorized. All other versions were destroyed.

Muslims consider the Qur'an to be the literal word of God, which was dictated to Muhammad and has never been altered. The other major monotheistic religions, Judaism and Christianity, also have sacred scriptures, but these are believed to have been written by humans inspired by God. Islam asserts that, while the Torah and the Christian Scriptures are also holy books, they have been changed over time. Unlike the Bible, the Qur'an is protected by God from manipulation or distortion.

Muslims believe that humans would be unable to produce anything like the Qur'an. This characteristic of the Qur'an is called its *inimitability,* and it is based on the belief of its divine authorship. Because the Qur'an is God's word, Muslims devote much time to studying its content and use of language. It is the most important source of Islamic spiritual doctrine.

The Qur'an contains 114 chapters, called *suras*. After the first chapter, the suras are organized according to length, from the longest to the shortest. The first chapter is called al-Fatiha ("The

The Qur'an, Islam's most important text, contains God's revelations to all mankind. It is broken into chapters, called suras; this illuminated page from the Qur'an shows Sura 96.

Opening"), and it is a short chapter that Muslims recite during each of their five daily prayers. Every chapter is divided into verses called *ayat*. Chapters in the Qur'an address a variety of issues, including God and creation, Muhammad as a spiritual and political leader, other prophets, Islam as a faith, human responsibility and reasoning, and God's requirements for society in general.

While the Qur'an is the basis of law and doctrine for Islam, it does not contain much information about specific religious practices for Muslims. For example, while it prescribes prayer, it does not elaborate on exactly how a Muslim should pray. Many of the specific religious practices associated with Islam are derived from the Hadith, Muhammad's sayings and practices.

THE HADITH AND THE SUNNA

The Companions recorded Muhammad's statements, religious instructions, assertions, and actions. Collectively these are called the Hadith. They are second only to the Qur'an as a source of Islamic doctrine and practice. Each separate story is also called a Hadith. The Hadith are important because they provide the real-life context of Muhammad's daily existence to illustrate how the tenets presented in the Qur'an apply to the believers's daily life.

Unlike the Qur'an, there is no absolute canon of Hadith. Many Hadith have been preserved, but some are considered inaccurate; others are accepted by certain Muslim sects but not by others. To eliminate Hadith that did not really originate with Muhammad, Muslim scholars and jurists developed elaborate standards to help determine the authenticity of each Hadith. They examined the contents of the sayings, as well as the reliability of the Companions with whom they originated and the narrators who passed on the stories. By the ninth century, approximately 250 years after Muhammad's death, Muslim scholars had compiled four sets of Hadith that are considered legitimate. These were collected, checked, validated, and compiled by Muhammad Ibn Ismail al-Bukhari (809–870), Muslim Ibn al-Hajjaj (817–876),

Sulaiman Ibn Ash'ath, also known as Abu Dawud (817–888), and Muhammad Ibn Zayid (824–915).

The sets compiled by two scholars are considered the most authoritative. Al-Bukhari, the best known collector of sound Hadith, analyzed approximately a half-million sayings and validated the authenticity of only 7,500. Each saying that Muslim Ibn al-Hajjaj validated is supposed to be directly traceable to someone who either heard what Muhammad said or who witnessed what Muhammad did.

In addition, Hadith compiled by Imam Malik (715–795), Abu Muhammad al-Husain Ibn Mas'ud (d. 1122), and Ahmad Ibn Hanbal (780–885) are only accepted by some Muslims "For example, the eponym of the Hanabali law school, Ahmad Ibn Hanbal, was a great collector of Hadith, but his standards of criticism were not considered sufficiently rigorous, so his collection has never won full acceptance from the other law-schools," writes John Alden Williams.

The Hadith are important because they provide specific religious and social guidance that Muslims may apply to their daily lives. The example of Muhammad, as revealed through the Hadith, is known as the *Sunna* (Arabic for "path"). For example, the Qur'an tells Muslims that they have certain obligations: to be charitable to others, to perform daily prayers, to pay a tax for the benefit of the Muslim state, and to make decisions as a community. The ways in which these things should be done are found in the Sunna.

THE FIVE PILLARS OF ISLAM

Islam's five fundamental obligations include the profession of faith (*shahada*), daily prayer (*salat*), almsgiving (*zakat*), fasting during the month of Ramadan (*sawm*), and the pilgrimage to Mecca (*hajj*).

Allah, the all-knowing, all-powerful, and all-merciful God, is central to Islam. By professing God's uniqueness, submitting to His will, and respecting the commandments He gave to Muhammad,

Muslims pray around the Kaaba, an ancient shrine in Mecca, during the annual *hajj*, or pilgrimage. Whenever Muslims throughout the world make their daily prayers, they are expected to face in the direction of the Kaaba.

Muslims demonstrate their appreciation for God's nature, the miracle of creation, and God's plan for His creation. Therefore, the profession of faith is a prerequisite for anyone who wishes to join the Muslim community. Muslims profess their faith during their daily prayers, saying each time, "I bear witness that there is no god but Allah and that Muhammad is His messenger." While a person's actions may be scrutinized in the Muslim community, his or her profession of faith is enough to gain entrance into the community and may not be challenged by anyone.

The second pillar of Islam involves a Muslim's duty to say five prescribed daily prayers—at dawn, noon, mid-afternoon, sunset, and evening. All adult Muslims are required to cleanse and purify themselves before performing their prayers. During the early days of Islam, Muslims were required to face Jerusalem while praying, but they were later instructed to face the Kaaba, an ancient shrine located in Mecca. For Muslims, the Kaaba represents the continuity and unity of the divine message. To this day, Muslims face in the direction of Mecca during prayer.

Each prayer is composed of a series of units, called *rak'a*, which involves standing, kneeling, and prostrating. The worshiper performs these sequences of movements while reciting passages from the Qur'an, along with some prayers that do not originate directly from it. The noon and afternoon prayers (*zuhr* and *'asr*) consist of four *rak'as* each; the sunset prayers (*maghrib*), three *rak'as* each; and the dawn and night prayers (*fajr* and *isha*), two *rak'as* each. The first chapter of the Qur'an, al-Fatiha, is recited during each unit of a prayer sequence, and every prayer ends with the repetition of the profession of faith and the benediction, "May the peace, mercy, and blessings of God be upon you."

While Muslims are encouraged to pray in mosques, or places of worship, they are required to pray in groups only one time per week, at noon on Friday. A religious leader, called an imam, leads the congregational prayer. At other times Muslims may pray individually or in groups wherever they want. At the mosque, worshipers arrange themselves in rows so that they may kneel and bow without touching anyone around them. In some Muslim communities, women pray separately from men.

The third pillar of Islam is the obligation of Muslims to help the poor. The requirement that Muslims must share with those who are destitute to help raise them out of poverty is stressed throughout the Qur'an. There are two forms of charitable giving: a mandatory tax (*zakat*) and voluntary almsgiving (*sadaqa*). However, the Qur'an does not contain specific guidelines for how much one should give or how this obligation should be enforced. The amount and manner of giving have been the subject of much debate and study over the centuries. Muslims were traditionally taxed on their earnings, as well as their savings and possessions.

"In the early Islamic state, the *zakat* was the only tax paid by Muslims, was used for community purposes and together with the taxes levied on non-Muslims made up the revenue of the state," explains John Alden Williams. "While a few of the ultra-orthodox still regard these taxes and land tax as the only taxes a Muslim government can legally levy, *zakat* is usually treated today as an obligation to spend money for charitable purposes and is hardly distinguished from almsgiving."

The fourth pillar of Islam is the fast during the month of Ramadan. Ramadan is one of the 12 months of the Islamic lunar calendar. Because the lunar calendar follows the phases of the moon rather than the earth's revolution around the sun, the length of a year is 354 or 355 days, 10 or 11 days shorter than the Western 365-day calendar. Therefore, Ramadan begins on different dates each year. Ramadan is considered a sacred month because it was during this month that Muhammad received his first revelations from God.

During Ramadan, Muslims must refrain from eating and other pleasures from daybreak to sundown each day. People who are sick, pregnant, or traveling may be exempted from fasting but are required to make up the missed days later. Those people who are unable to make up the missed days, such as the terminally ill, pay alms for each missed day of fasting.

The purpose of the fast is to practice physical and spiritual discipline, to serve as a reminder of the trials of the poor, and to build a sense of solidarity among all Muslims. Muslims may decide to fast at other times of the year, but this is not required. At the end of Ramadan, worshipers celebrate with a three-day holiday of breaking the fast that is known as Eid al-Fitr.

The fifth pillar of Islam calls for all Muslims who have the physical and financial ability to make a pilgrimage to Mecca at least once in their lives. Muslims from all walks of life make the

A colorful selection of Ramadan lanterns hangs in a shop in Cairo, Egypt. Ramadan, the ninth month of the Islamic lunar calendar, is a time of fasting and self-sacrifice for Muslims.

journey to Mecca; for this reason the *hajj* is considered one of the most unifying experiences of the Islamic faith. While details of the actual journey and visit to Mecca may vary—some pilgrims stay in tents near the city, while other stay in luxury hotels—all Muslims who make the pilgrimage are considered equal before God. The spiritual objective of the pilgrimage to Mecca is to set aside worldly concerns and to commune with God.

Because Islam prohibited depictions of Allah—and, in some cases, of human forms—Muslim artists found other ways to decorate buildings and books. (Top) An example of ornate tile work from an African mosque. (Inset) An American Muslim carefully works on a calligraphic design.

ISLAMIC THEOLOGY

Theology is the study of God, His nature, attributes, relationship to the universe, and other such questions. For centuries, Muslim theologians have investigated God's nature and His attributes, including justice and mercy. Mainstream Muslims consider God an entity beyond human comprehension or direct perception. (This view was rejected by a number of Islamic movements, including Mutazilism and Sufism.) God is thought to be entirely unique and transcendent, a complete "other." (As the supreme being God has no gender, but Muslims traditionally refer to Him with masculine pronouns.) Muslims believe, however, that God and his powers may be seen and felt in His creation of the universe and that, through reflection, people may recognize God's wisdom.

Because humans cannot understand God, Islamic law does not permit them to depict Him in drawings, paintings, sculpture, or other artwork. Representations of Muhammad are generally also forbidden; some Muslims believe the human figure itself should never be depicted. Images or icons of God, Muhammad, or the saints could lead some people to worship them as idols, a practice strictly forbidden in Islam. Because of the restrictions, over the centuries Muslim artists focused their creativity in other ways, such as the creation of decorative tile patterns and ornate calligraphy.

The Qur'an mentions 28 messengers from God who lived before Muhammad. In addition, Muslims believe God sent thousands of prophets to people around the world in the time before his final message was revealed through Muhammad. According to Islamic doctrine, God revealed to Muhammad the perfect code of faith—one that combines spiritual teachings and commandments. This is the final message from God, and Muslims believe this code supplants Jewish and Christian doctrines and will meet humanity's needs for the rest of eternity.

To Muslims, God, as creator and sustainer, never abandons the things that He creates, and sending prophets is God's way of providing people with the guidance they need to achieve salvation, both in this world and in the afterworld. In addition, Muslims believe that God is just and that His sense of fairness requires Him to send prophets to act as examples of how to live, as He holds people accountable for their actions and beliefs.

Muslims believe God created the world for the benefit of humankind and that God constantly shows His mercy for His people by dedicating all of creation for their service. God's mercy for humankind is also manifested in the status that He awards people in the world, as Muslims believe God appointed people to be His caliphs, or viceroys, on earth, trusting them to fulfill His plan for creation.

Islamic beliefs are different from the Judeo-Christian tradition that Adam and Eve, the first people, were punished after they sinned by disobeying God. Christians believe that everyone is born with original sin on his or her soul, and that people receive redemption through Jesus Christ, who was crucified in order to save humanity. By contrast, the Qur'an indicates that God forgave Adam and Eve when they repented of their sin, and He entrusted them to act as guardians of the earth. Because in Islamic theology there is no original sin, Muslims believe that Jesus was not required to die on the cross to redeem the sins of humanity. Muslims view Jesus as a prophet with an important message from God to all humanity, but they reject the idea that Jesus is the Son of God. To Muslims, the concept of the "Holy Trinity" is a contradiction of the oneness of God.

Debates among Muslim theologians have refined the Muslims' concept of God throughout the centuries. For example, in order to avoid comparing God to the beings He created, some theologians have argued that, when the Qur'an attributes human-like qualities to God (like those related to the five senses), it is doing so metaphorically. Another important question that Muslim theologians have argued is that of free will and predestination—the idea that God has predetermined all actions and worldly events. One group of theologians argued that God creates only good, as otherwise his punishment of misbehaving humans would not be fair. Other Muslim theologians rejected this notion on the argument that it limits God's capabilities, which according to the Qur'an is not possible.

MYSTICISM IN ISLAM

Sufism is a form of mysticism that first emerged late in the seventh century C.E. It was the product of a variety of influences, not the least of which is a mystical tone in some of the teachings of Muhammad. One of the primary influences was the Qur'an itself, which contains many mystical verses. Sufism was also influenced

A group of Sufis in Konya, Turkey, perform a whirling dance called the Sema, through which they believe they can attain unity with God. These Sufis are followers of the philosopher and poet Mevlana Celaleddin Rumi, who founded a monastery in Konya.

by people's desire to escape the hardships accompanying the social and political upheavals of the time and by the desire to live quieter, more spiritual lives—a reaction to the extravagant lifestyles of the early Umayyad caliphs. Some have also attributed the emergence and development of Islamic mysticism to external influences, such as Indian, Persian, and especially Greek thought, prevalent in the territories that were added to the Islamic state within ten years after Muhammad's death. Though there are different points of view regarding the orgin and meaning of the word "sufi," the general view is that the word is derived from the Arabic word *suf*, which means "wool," because the first practitioners of Islamic mysticism wore woolen robes similar to those worn by Christian monks. However, Sufis do not make up a separate Islamic sect. Most are Sunni Muslims, and they consider Sufism to be a practice within mainstream Islam.

Sufis believe that one can have knowledge of God and a personal relationship with Him. Accordingly, the Sufi mystic—sometimes self-described as a pilgrim on a journey—follows a path to spiritual enlightenment that leads to attaining knowledge and direct relationship with God. According to some Sufi orders (*tariqas*), this journey has seven stages: repentance, abstinence, renunciation, poverty, patience, trust in God, and acquiescence to the will of God. But the number and arrangement of these steps differ from one order to another. Regardless, these steps together form the human stage and are referred to as *Maqamat* (stations). Once the mystic has gone through all stations, he or she acquires a higher level of consciousness through the grace of God. This divinely given stage is referred to as *ahwal* (states).

Some early mystics, such as al-Bistami (d. 858) and al-Hallaj (d. 922) believed that through their mystical experience, it was possible to have direct union with God, and that it was not possible to express with words this matchless experience of union. Those who did try to express it scandalized other Muslims by loudly and boldly declaring their identity with God. Furthermore, while most early Sufis carefully observed the traditional religious laws, some did not, angering their Muslim peers and religious leaders.

In the late 11th and early 12th centuries, the Islamic theologian al-Ghazali (d. 1111) reconciled traditional Islam to mysticism. He argued that the individual should try to obtain a mystical experience with God, but that Sufis must also try to live in peace with others in the Muslim community. Within a century after al-Ghazali's death, the Islamic community accepted this interpretation of Islam, which emphasized the individual's personal, emotional relationship to God. At that point, Sufism became a strong force, winning for Islam many new converts, particularly in central Asia.

As time progressed, Sufism became more formal in nature, and individual mystics attracted groups of followers who wanted to pursue the mystic's path, or *tariqa*—a set of mental and physical exercises designed to help one develop the direct experience with God. Eventually, the term tariqa came to mean any group of people following a particular Sufi mystic. Sometimes such groups became like monastic organizations.

Sufi orders or brotherhoods came to be called *tariqas*, although it was not until the 12th and 13th centuries that they became stable enough to survive the deaths of their founders. This was achieved by the founder personally nominating a successor, and thus some orders today can trace their lineage back more than 700 years.

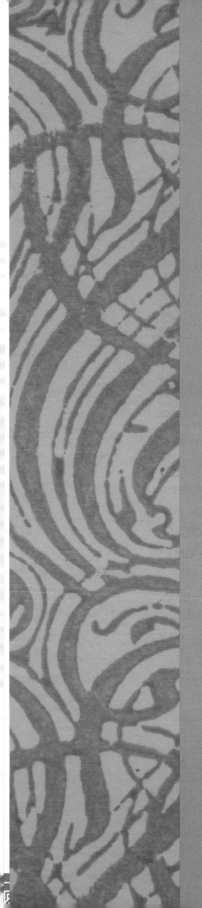

A book of Islamic legal opinions, dating from 808, is open on a shelf in the Khalidi Library, Jerusalem. The interpretation of Islamic law has an important effect on the everyday lives of all Muslims.

Islamic Legal Sources

One basic principle that may be gleaned from the Qur'an and from the example of Muhammad's life is that Islam is based both on behavior and on belief. Muslims are expected to believe only in Allah, to follow His teachings, and to behave in a prescribed way. They must submit to the code of conduct God delivered through Muhammad. Islam tells its followers how to live in a way that is pleasing to God. The principles of social justice, individual dignity, and shared peace within the community are paramount. Muslims must adhere to regulations concerning daily life, commerce, and relations within the family and with the greater society. Because of this, Islam is considered a way of life. A consequence of this is that the study of law is more important to the ordinary Muslim than the study of theology.

Sharia may be found in the relationship between religious and secular law and the extent to which they influence each other. With the exception of Saudi Arabia, where a strict version of Sharia is the basis for all laws, what generally occurs in Muslim countries is that Sharia principles apply to domestic matters and to matters regarding the society's moral code, while secular matters are left for the secular governments to address. Thus Sharia provides the moral foundation of society, and it is applied to secular matters only to the extent that it ensures secular laws do not clash with it.

In some Middle Eastern countries, such as Jordan, Morocco, and Turkey, the state's legal system is secular, rather than Sharia-based. Other Muslim countries, such as Pakistan and Malaysia, do include Sharia courts as an important part of their legal system. In

Two women wearing the veiled garment known as the *hijab* walk past the Sharia Court in Katsina, a town in northern Nigeria. Sharia has played a prominent—and highly divisive—role in the Nigerian legal system, as has been the case in Sudan and several other African countries.

Egypt the constitution was amended in 1979 so that the Sharia was made "the basis" rather than "a basis" for legislation in that country. In Sudan the imposition of Sharia as the basis of law was an important contributor to the long-running civil war between Muslims and Christians that has cost an estimated 2 million lives.

Some westerners have argued that Sharia is an outdated legal system that should be changed to reflect contemporary approaches to justice and punishment. A particular area of complaint are punishments widely considered to be barbaric, such as the severing of limbs, stoning, hanging, and flogging. Many Muslims, however, point out that Sharia is a moral code—one for which there are various interpretations—and explain that Sharia is much more than its controversial punishments. "When people think about Sharia law, they often think about the penalties for certain crimes," Imam Feisal Abdul Rauf of Masjid al-Farah in New York City told the television program *Frontline*. "They don't think about the sum total of Islamic law and its jurisprudence, which means the underlying structure and philosophy and understanding of how you arrive at what we call the Islamically correct decision. You do not define Sharia law by just a couple of penalties."

A mosque in Kuala Lumpur, the capital of Malaysia. Most of Malaysia's 23 million people are Muslims.

The Distribution of Muslims Today

Today there are about 1.25 billion Muslims living throughout the world, and Islam continues to grow faster than any other religion. Even though Muslims worldwide feel united as a community of believers, there are many differences in doctrine and practice within the Islamic world. Although all followers of Islam share a core set of beliefs, political, geographic, and ethnic diversity account for a variety of accepted Islamic practices. Indonesian Muslims have certain practices that differ from those of Iranian or Kuwaiti Muslims, for example.

As the Islamic world enters the 21st century, the physical settings and human conditions in which Islam is prevalent have changed dramatically. Most Muslims live in nation-states created in the aftermath of the long period of European colonialism, and these states were given, or earned, independence at a time when exciting advances in technology were being developed. Thus, Muslims in even the most remote areas were exposed to new ideas and experiences as the 20th century progressed. More important, countries that were freed from colonial rule had the opportunity to choose what sort of government they wanted. Islam provided its followers with general rules and practices that could be used to help shape their societies.

To Muslims, the tenets of Islam are immutable, yet the Qur'an contains few specific guidelines regarding the practice of faith in a rapidly changing world. Thus Islam provides believers with a

A crowd of people waves on a street in Dhaka, the capital of Bangladesh. Islam is the dominant religion in Bangladesh; 83 percent of the country's citizens—more than 115 million people—are Muslims.

sense of spiritual security along with the flexibility to adapt to modern conditions. As Muslims strike off on unfamiliar paths, students, politicians, scholars, and essayists in most Islamic countries work to guarantee that Islam's social and religious traditions are not lost. They urge their peers to embrace their own Islamic heritage, and, in doing so, they help to solidify Islam's place in the modern world without necessarily rejecting the advances of the modern world.

Cultural differences are the cause of many social controversies within Islam. This is especially evident in the debate over the role of women in society. Today, the rights women in the Islamic world enjoy vary widely from country to country. In some places women possess very little social and economic independence. In other countries, such as Bangladesh, Malaysia, Pakistan, Turkey, and Tunisia, women have many more rights and may serve as government officials.

Today, Muslims live in almost every country of the world. An increasing number of nations have growing Muslim populations, and many countries in Asia, Africa, and the Middle East are composed almost entirely of Muslims.

ISLAM IN ASIA

Asia is the largest continent, covering 30 percent of the world's total land area. It is also the world's most populous continent, with nearly three-fifths of all people. Islam is the dominant religion in many countries of Asia, and the daily lives of Muslims who live in this region are unique. Such countries as India, Indonesia, Bangladesh, Pakistan, Malaysia, and Singapore all have significant Muslim populations.

Central Asia contains some of the most populous Islamic nations. In countries such as Pakistan (156 million people), Iran (68 million), and Afghanistan (28 million), nearly all of the people are Muslims. Islam is also the majority religion in a number of small states that were once part of the Soviet Union. In the largest of these, Uzbekistan, 22 million people (or 88 percent of the country's total population) are Muslim. In Kyrgyzstan 75 percent of the approximately 5 million people are Muslim; 90 percent of Tajikistan's 6.4 million people are followers of Islam, as are 89 percent of Turkmenistan's 4.7 million citizens. In another former Soviet state, Kazakhstan, Muslims constitute a plurality of the people (47 percent, compared with 44 percent Orthodox Christians).

Significant Muslim communities exist in Asian countries where other religions dominate. India, for example, has the world's second-largest population at more than 1 billion people. Although Muslims make up just 12 percent of the country's total population, there are more than 120 million Indian Muslims—more Muslims than live on the Arabian Peninsula. Nepal is the only state in which Hinduism is the official religion, yet an estimated 4 percent of its population is Muslim.

Islam had spread as far east as China by the eighth century, but there are fewer Muslims living in eastern Asia. China has a Muslim population of between 20 million and 26 million people. (This communist country is officially atheist.) There are also small Muslim communities in Japan, South Korea, and Mongolia.

Southeast Asia is home to several countries in which a majority of the people are Muslims. These include Indonesia (the world's largest Muslim nation, with more than 205 million adherents of Islam), Malaysia, and Brunei. About 14 percent of Singapore's 3.8 million people follow Islam; most of these people are the ethnic Malays who live in the country. The Philippines also has a significant Muslim population of about 4.25 million, approximately 5 percent of the country's total population. Burma (also called Myanmar), Vietnam, and Thailand are home to smaller communities of Muslims.

Asia gave birth to some of the world's oldest civilizations, and today many Asians are followers of the ancient religions Hinduism and Buddhism. Asians practice a variety of other local religions, as well as Christianity to a limited degree. Against this backdrop of religious diversity, numerous conflicts involving Muslims have occurred over the years. For instance, India (where most of the population is Hindu) and Pakistan (where Muslims make up the overwhelming majority) have fought several wars over the Kashmir territory. Muslims constitute a majority in this province of India, and, many of them want to become a part of Pakistan. However, India has controlled Kashmir since the modern states of India and Pakistan were created in 1947. The dispute over this territory continues to be a major source of tension in the region, and the consequences of a full-scale war between India and Pakistan would be grave, as both countries have nuclear weapons.

Muslim women display a banner during a January 2004 rally in Srinagar, a city in the disputed Kashmir province of India. Unrest over Kashmir, where Muslims are a majority, has caused more than a half-century of tension between Pakistan and India.

But conflict involving Muslims in Southeast Asia is not restricted to India and Pakistan. The Muslim Moro people who live on Mindanao Island in the Philippines have fought for years with their government, arguing for greater sovereignty and for closer relations with the Muslims who live in Malaysia's state of Sabah. In 1996 the Philippine government and the largest rebel group reached an agreement that created an autonomous region for the Muslims, but smaller rebel groups have continued the fight.

In the largely Muslim parts of Asia, religious groups are often responsible for elementary school instruction. However, the number of students who attend school varies quite dramatically throughout Asia. In most Asian countries, the great majority of young children attend elementary (or primary) school, because their governments emphasize the importance of such schooling. Thus, all children attend elementary school in Sri Lanka, Indonesia, and Burma. However, in some countries, such as Bangladesh and Pakistan, only 50 to 75 percent of the children receive a primary education, and most of the children who do attend school are boys. Generally speaking, secondary-school enrollment is comparatively low throughout Asia, and proportionally even fewer of those students go on to attend universities.

ISLAM IN EUROPE

The great majority of Europe's people in Christians, and Roman Catholics form the single largest religious group in the region. Two European countries that are predominantly Islamic, however, are Turkey and Albania.

Russia, too, has a large Muslim population; in fact, with about 20 million believers, Islam is second only to the Orthodox Christian Church as the country's largest religious group. In Russia, Muslims are found in the greatest concentrations in the republics of Tatarstan and Bashkortostan in the middle Volga region, and in the republics of Chechnya,

Ingushetia, Alania (North Ossetia), Kabardino-Balkaria, and Dagestan. Because Islam is a relatively popular religion in Russia, Muslims in the country don't generally experience significant problems with their non-Muslim neighbors or with the government.

Although the communist government of the Soviet Union did not permit Muslims to worship freely, today the Russian government recognizes Islam as a religion that was part of the country's historical development. Therefore, Islam is permitted to spread and develop within the country, unhindered by laws that restrict the

Russian president Vladimir Putin is pictured on huge television screens as he addresses the opening session of the Organization of the Islamic Conference (OIC) summit, October 2003. A statement issued by the Kremlin noted that Putin's attendance at the conference underscored "the importance for Russia, a large number of whose inhabitants practice Islam, to be present at this prestigious forum." The OIC is an association of 56 Islamic states that was formed in 1969 to promote Muslim unity on economic, social, and political affairs.

growth of any religion other than Christianity, Islam, Judaism, or Buddhism. In 2003 the Russian government indicated that it was interested in joining the Organization of the Islamic Conference (OIC), a group of 56 countries that have Muslim majorities or large Muslim populations.

Albania is a small country in eastern Europe with a majority Muslim population—of its 3.6 million residents, about 70 percent are Muslim and 30 percent are Christian. As in the Soviet Union,

The Blue Mosque, built in the early 17th century at the order of an Ottoman sultan, is one of the most famous buildings in Istanbul, Turkey. Today, Turkey has the largest Muslim population of Europe. Since the formation of the modern state from the ruins of the Ottoman Empire after the end of World War I, Turkey's leaders have been careful to keep religion out of government affairs.

communists ruled Albania for many years, and in 1967 all of the country's mosques and churches were closed and religious services were prohibited. The communist government in Albania collapsed in 1989, and in the early 1990s democratic and economic reforms were instituted. At first, the tremendous disruption brought on by the change in government led to a steep economic decline that included high rates of unemployment and widespread poverty. However, from 1993 to 1995 Albania's economy recovered rapidly, due mostly to a recovery in the farming industry. Though Albania now relies much less on foreign aid than in the years directly following the decline of communism, the country still relies on thousands of Albanians who work in Greece, Italy, and Germany to send money home to support their families. Although living conditions for most Albanians have improved, poverty remains widespread.

There are not significant religious divisions in Albania—often, members of a single family practice different faiths. Education is mandatory for children between the ages of 6 and 14. In 1996 almost all school-age children attended elementary school, but only 35 percent attended high school. Literacy rates are comparatively high in Albania—approximately 86 percent of the adult population can read and write.

Turkey—which actually is situated between Europe and Asia—claims the largest Muslim population in Europe, with about 67 million followers of Islam. The modern state of Turkey was founded in 1923 out of the ruins of the Ottoman Empire. From the beginning, nationalist leaders like Kemal Atatürk established the government on a secular basis; religious laws and leaders were given no preference in the new state. This closely enforced policy of secularism has resulted in problems. Although many residents of Turkey seem to prefer the separation of mosque and state, some Islamic fundamentalists argue that Sharia and Islamic values should play a much greater role in the government's operation.

Turkey is a key ally of the United States and other Western

nations. An important member of the North Atlantic Treaty Organization, it is also NATO's only Muslim country. Turkey has a dynamic economy and has developed along Western lines. Its educational system has also improved greatly over the years. In 1923 fully 90 percent of adults were illiterate. Today, thanks to compulsory education, 79 percent of adults can read and write.

To Turkey's northwest lies Europe's Balkan Peninsula, which is home to several nations with significant Muslim minorities. Bulgaria, with which Turkey shares a border, has a total population of more than 7.5 million, about 12 percent of whom follow Islam. Muslims account for about 3 in 10 residents of the former Yugoslav republic of Macedonia, whose total population exceeds 2 million. Serbia and Montenegro's population of approximately 10.7 million includes more than 2 million Muslims, about 19 percent of the country's people. Four in 10 of Bosnia and Herzegovina's approximately 4 million citizens are Muslims.

During the 1990s, the Balkan Peninsula was the site of bloody fighting fueled, at least in part, by animosity between Muslims and Christians. In the decades after World War II, the Federal Republic of Yugoslavia—an ethnically and religiously diverse country—had been unified by the authoritarian regime of its communist leader, Josip Broz Tito, and by fear of Soviet domination. But after Tito's death in 1980 and the collapse of the Soviet Union 11 years later, nationalist sentiments began to bubble up in Yugoslavia's six republics. After the republics of Slovenia, Croatia, and Macedonia declared their independence from Yugoslavia in 1991, Bosnia and Herzegovina followed suit in 1992. Bosnia and Herzegovina was Yugoslavia's most ethnically balanced republic, with Slavic Muslims (Bosniaks) constituting about 44 percent of its population, predominantly Orthodox Christian Serbs making up an additional 31 percent, and predominantly Roman Catholic Croats accounting for 17 percent. Yet the three groups could not agree on Bosnia's future.

Bosnian Muslims and Croats voted for independence in a referendum boycotted by Bosnian Serbs. Then, following the official declaration of independence on March 3, 1992, fighting erupted as Yugoslavia's Serb-dominated army joined Bosnian Serbs in a brutal campaign to drive Muslims out of large swaths of Bosnia. The ultimate goal of the genocidal campaign, euphemistically called "ethnic cleansing," was to unite the Republic of Serbia with Serb-controlled territories in Bosnia, thereby creating a "Greater Serbia." The plan's mastermind, many observers believe, was Slobodan Milosevic, Serbia's communist leader.

The Serb forces had the advantage of much better arms, and Bosniaks bore the brunt of the three-year-long conflict: 90 percent of the approximately 200,000 people killed in the fighting were Muslims, and most of them were civilians. In addition, the war created about a million Bosnian refugees and internally displaced persons.

Initially, efforts by the international community to stop the killing proved ineffectual. The United Nations dispatched peacekeeping troops and in 1993 established six "safe areas" where Muslims would supposedly be protected from Serb aggression, but shelling of these areas continued. A 1994 Serb mortar attack on Sarajevo, the Bosnian capital, claimed 68 lives and left more than 200 wounded. The following year, Serbian forces overran the U.N.-declared safe areas of Srebrenica and Zepa. In Srebrenica, a small mining town, they massacred more than 7,000 Muslim men and boys. The atrocity, Europe's worst massacre since World War II, spurred U.S. and NATO intervention. After enduring a month-long NATO bombing campaign, Serbian leaders agreed to a ceasefire, and in November 1995 the U.S.-mediated Dayton Accord finally brought the conflict to an end. But among many Muslims worldwide, resentment lingers over the slow response of Western governments in protecting Bosnian Muslims against Christian aggressors.

In western Europe, several countries, including France, the United Kingdom, and Germany, have significant Muslim populations. In

French Muslims walk through the garden at a mosque in Paris. France's proximity to Muslim North Africa and its colonial ties to Algeria contributed to the growth of a Muslim population that is now the largest in Western Europe.

some cases, this is a reflection of the colonial heritage of these countries. France, for example, ruled large parts of North Africa during the 19th century and the first half of the 20th century. Algeria, one of the largest countries in Africa, won its freedom from French rule in 1961 after a bloody eight-year-long war for independence. However, Algeria underwent its own devastating civil war during the 1990s, and many Muslims immigrated to France to avoid the violence. Today, France has a Muslim community numbered at about 5 million people.

Britain's Muslim population, which today stands at more than a million, can be traced in part to its long-time involvement in the Middle East and Asia. Many Muslim Indians, Pakistanis, and Arabs are drawn to the United Kingdom by its educational opportunities.

Many of the Muslims living in Germany today are immigrants from Turkey. Though it has a strong manufacturing base, Germany has suffered shortages of workers, and Turkish Muslims have seen an opportunity to take good-paying jobs. Today, the Muslim population of Germany is estimated at more than 3 million, or about 3.7 percent of Europe's most populous country.

Even countries in which the Roman Catholic Church is very strong, such as Spain and Italy, are attracting Muslim immigrants. It is estimated that there are Muslim communities of between 500,000 and 800,000 people in each of those countries. There are also significant Muslim communities in Sweden, Belgium, Denmark, Norway, and the Netherlands. And the official numbers do not take into account undocumented, or illegal, Muslim immigrants to these countries.

ISLAM IN THE MIDDLE EAST

Most of the countries in the region historically known as the Middle East—the Arabian Peninsula and eastern Mediterranean—are ethnically Arab. Countries in which 90 percent or more of the population follows Islam include Bahrain (about 660,000 people), Iraq (24 million), Jordan (5.3 million), Kuwait (2.1 million), Oman (2.7 million), Qatar (793,000), Saudi Arabia (23.5 million), Syria (17 million), the United Arab Emirates (2.5 million), and Yemen (18.7 million).

The Jewish state of Israel is the only country in the Middle East that does not have a majority Muslim population. There are about 6.1 million people living in Israel; about 80 percent are Jewish, while about 15 percent are Muslim. (Israel also has a small Christian population.) Large Muslim populations of Palestinian Arabs live in territories occupied by Israel: 75 percent of the West Bank's 2.2 million people are Palestinian Muslims, as are more than 98 percent of the Gaza Strip's 1.3 million people.

Lebanon, just north of Israel, is home to more than 3.7 million people. About 70 percent of the population is Muslim, while 30 percent is Christian. However, for many years Lebanon was ruled under an agreement that gave Christians a greater share of power in the government. In 1975 a civil war broke out, dividing the country along political lines and reducing much of Lebanon's cosmopolitan capital, Beirut, into rubble. The fighting continued for 16 years, until the 1991 Taif Accord established a basis for peace. In part, the Accord gives Muslims a greater say in government than before, and addressed other issues, such as education.

A number of resistance movements grew out of the continuing Arab/Israeli conflict in the Middle East. For example, the Lebanese Islamist organization Hezbollah ("Party of God") was formed to oppose a 1982 Israeli invasion of Lebanon. This Shiite organization, which combines social activism with military resistance, has grown into a political power in Lebanon, where it currently controls a bloc of seats in the country's parliament. Hezbollah has gained support from the people of southern Lebanon by establishing a network of schools, mosques, and medical clinics, and by providing charitable assistance to people in need. Additionally, to pursue its goal of driving Israel out of every part of Lebanon, the Party continues to resist militarily and apply force against Israel.

Another group that has used military force to further its political agenda is the militant Palestinian organization Hamas. Like Hezbollah, Hamas has established a network that provides social services to many Palestinians, both within the occupied West Bank and Gaza Strip territories and in the Palestinian refugee camps located in Jordan and other neighboring Arab states. In an attempt to put an end to Israel's occupation of Palestinian terri-

A Lebanese man watches a rushing stream flow through a park near Beirut. About 70 percent of Lebanon's 3.8 million people are Muslims, while 30 percent are Christian.

Arab Muslims go about their business near the Damascus Gate, East Jerusalem. The establishment of the state of Israel in 1948, and Israel's occupation of the West Bank and Gaza Strip territories since 1967, has been a constant source of tension in the Middle East.

tories, Hamas plans and carries out suicide bombing attacks against military as well as civilian targets inside Israel. These attacks have killed hundreds of Israelis, leading to violent reprisals by the Israeli military against the Palestinians—reprisals that, in turn, have killed hundreds of Palestinians, many of whom were civilians. These attacks and counterattacks contributed greatly to the collapse of the Arab-Israeli peace process in 2000.

Conflict in the Middle East is not restricted to Palestine, however. In the summer of 1990, Iraq invaded its smaller neighbor Kuwait. The United States and its allies sent military forces to Saudi Arabia to help defend it against a possible Iraqi invasion. In

January 1991, a multinational coalition led by the United States launched the Gulf War against Iraq, forcing the armies of Saddam Hussein out of Kuwait in six weeks of fighting. Another war involving Iraq broke out in March 2003, when the United States invaded the country. As justification for the invasion, the Bush administration cited Iraq's refusal to comply fully with its obligations to dismantle its nuclear-, chemical-, and biological-weapons programs, a requirement imposed by the armistice agreement that ended the 1991 Gulf War. By April coalition forces had seized Baghdad, the capital of Iraq, forcing Hussein into hiding. However, some Iraqis continued to resist the U.S. occupation, and a campaign of guerrilla attacks and bombings had soon caused more U.S. casualties than were sustained during the combat phase of the war.

ISLAM IN AFRICA

Islam was introduced throughout northern Africa in the 600s, and in following centuries it spread along the eastern African coast and through the grasslands of western Africa. Today, in Egypt, Algeria, Morocco, Tunisia, Libya, Mauritania, and the disputed Western Sahara territory, more than 95 percent of the people follow Islam. Egypt is home to the largest number of Muslims in the region, with more than 70 million; it is followed by Algeria (32.5 million), Morocco (31.3 million), Tunisia (9.7 million), Libya (5.4 million), Mauritania (2.9 million), and the Western Sahara (about 262,000). In Sudan, to the south of Egypt, about 70 percent of the total population, or 26.6 million people, are followers of Islam. Islam is the state religion and Sharia the basis for laws in Sudan.

The North African countries have experienced many tensions. For example, the ethnic Berber minorities living in such countries as Morocco, Tunisia, and Algeria have long complained about discrimination by Arabs, who hold much of the power. This has led to unrest and violence. In Sudan the imposition of an Islamic government resulted in a long-running civil war that has led to more than 2 million deaths and the displacement of many indigenous people in the southern part of the country.

Islam is less rooted in central Africa, but that is not to say the Muslim presence in the region is inconsequential. Chad has a large Muslim community of over 4.7 million, more than half of the country's total population. However, like Sudan it has experienced ethnic, religious, and political violence since the mid-1960s. Most of the conflicts have been between Muslims living in the northern region of the country and the peoples of the southern region, the majority of whom follow traditional African religions or Christianity. Other countries of central Africa that have significant Muslim communities include the Democratic Republic of the Congo (5.6 million), Cameroon (3.15 million), Central African Republic (550,000), and Rwanda (360,000).

Islam spread into East Africa primarily through trade and missionary work during the eighth and ninth centuries. Many countries of East Africa have significant Muslim populations, including Ethiopia (33 million), Tanzania (12.6 million), Somalia (more than 8 million), and Uganda (4.1 million). The Muslim population of Kenya is not known for certain; estimates range from 3.2 million to nearly 8 million. Other countries with large Muslim communities are Malawi (2.3 million), Eritrea (2.2 million), Madagascar (1.2 million), and Djibouti (432,000).

In the countries of southern Africa, which were for many years British colonies, Christianity and native religions are much more common than is Islam. Zambia has the region's only large Muslim population, at about 2.4 million individuals, or nearly a quarter of the country's total population. By contrast, the proportion of Muslims in South Africa—the region's most populous nation with 42.8 million people—is less than 2 percent.

Islam is the major religion of West Africa. In Nigeria, the most populous country of Africa with more than 133 million people, about half are Muslims. Some states within Nigeria, particularly in the northern part of the country, have adopted Sharia laws. This

The Koutubia Mosque in Marrakech, Morocco, is a famous landmark. Nearly all of the people of Morocco are Muslims, but there has been unrest in the country because of differences between members of the Arab and Berber ethnic groups.

has caused friction between Muslims and non-Muslims, who feel the Sharia punishments are too harsh.

Muslims make up the majority in Burkina Faso (6.7 million Muslims, or 51 percent of the total population), the Gambia (1.35 million; 90 percent of the population), Guinea (7.65 million; 85 percent of the population), Mali (10.4 million; 90 percent of the population), Niger (8.8 million; 80 percent of the population), Senegal (9.87 million; 94 percent of the population), and Sierra Leone (3.4 million; about 60 percent of the population). There are also Muslim communities of significant size in Benin, Cote d'Ivoire, Ghana, Liberia, and Togo.

In general, the African countries face many problems. Most have been torn by war in the decades since receiving their independence from European imperial powers. South Africa is the only sub-Saharan country that can be classified as economically developed; even though many African nations possess valuable natural resources, in most cases mismanagement, corruption, or an absence of financial assets has stood in the way of economic development. Education is also a problem in Africa, and most adults in sub-Saharan Africa are illiterate. In many places, particularly in rural areas, there are shortages of schools, classroom materials, and qualified teachers. Quite a few children do not attend school at all, and others must leave school after a few years in order to help their families earn a living.

ISLAM IN THE AMERICAS

In the first years of the 21st century, an estimated 6 million Muslims were living in the United States, and Islam was the country's fastest-growing religion. Most U.S. Muslims are immigrants who arrived during the latter half of the 20th century, but approximately 30 percent are African Americans. Many of these African American Muslims have converted to Islam since the 1960s.

To the north of the United States, Canada is home to about 500,000 Muslims. To the south, Mexico has a Muslim population believed to be between 500,000 and 1 million.

For several centuries Roman Catholicism was the dominant religion of Latin America. In recent decades, however, Protestantism has made significant inroads, and the practice of Islam is growing more common in several South American and Caribbean countries. In Suriname about one in five citizens is a Muslim. Other countries in the region with significant Muslim communities include Guyana and the island nation of Trinidad and Tobago.

Iranian students demonstrate in support of their government during a 2003 rally at Tehran University. Iran is one of the few countries in which government is based solely on Islamic principles and laws.

Governments in the Islamic World

The 20th century saw the end of European colonialism in North Africa, the Middle East, and South Asia, where Islam's influence was broad and deep. One important result of this trend was the emergence of an Islamic fundamentalism that called for the creation of explicitly Islamic cultural and political alternatives to the secular governments and societies characteristic of the West.

THE IRANIAN REVOLUTION

From 1794 to 1925, shahs of the Qajar dynasty ruled Persia. Over the years, the Qajars' realm was encroached upon by European powers, particularly Russia and

Great Britain, which recognized Persia's strategic importance to their competing imperial interests. In 1906 a large backlash against foreign influence forced the shah to temporarily accept an elected legislature and a constitution. Soon, however, the shah disbanded the legislature and routed his opponents with the help of Russian troops. But by the end of World War I, Qajar rule was crumbling. In 1919 the British convinced the shah to accept the Anglo-Persian Agreement, making Persia a virtual British protectorate. The agreement spawned outrage among the citizens of Persia, and in 1921 a military officer named Reza Khan marched on Tehran and forced the shah to appoint him defense minister and, later, prime minister. By 1925 Reza Khan had put an end to the Qajar dynasty and declared himself shah, changing his name to Reza Shah Pahlavi. Thus was born a new Persian dynasty—the Pahlavis.

Persia was officially renamed Iran in 1935. Six years later, in the midst of World War II, the Soviet Union and Great Britain invaded the oil-rich country, professing concerns about the shah's overtures toward Nazi Germany, their enemy in the war. The invasion forced the shah into exile in South Africa, where he died. He was succeeded by his 22-year-old son, Mohammed Reza Pahlavi. During nearly four decades as Iran's shah, Mohammed Reza Pahlavi modernized the country. Staunchly anti-communist, he also forged a close relationship with the United States, using oil revenues to buy vast quantities of U.S. arms. But his authoritarian rule alienated many Iranians, and conservative Muslims objected to Western influences in the country.

Throughout the 1970s, Ayatollah Ruhollah Khomeini, a Shiite religious leader who had been expelled from Iran for criticizing the government and its policies, denounced the shah from exile. Khomeini's sermons—which called for the overthrow of the shah and the establishment of an Islamic state—were taped and smuggled into Iran, where they were distributed to sympathetic Shia imams. Khomeini also established a secret network of supporters within Iran.

During the late 1970s the Ayatollah Khomeini encouraged Iranians to overthrow the government of the shah and establish an Islamic state.

By the late 1970s Iran's economy was struggling, and dissatisfaction with the shah's regime spread across a broad spectrum of Iranian society. In 1978 street demonstrations and labor strikes swept Iran, and supporters of Khomeini cast the unrest as a struggle between Islam and the corrupt, un-Islamic, Western-oriented regime of the shah. In January 1979 the shah announced that he was leaving Iran for a short vacation, but he would never get the opportunity to return. On February 1, Khomeini returned to Tehran, where he was greeted by a large, enthusiastic crowd.

The ayatollah quickly set about dismantling the remnants of the shah's regime, stamping out Western influences, and consolidating the control of the Islamic Revolution. The monarchy of the shahs was replaced with a republican form of government that incorporated the principles of Shiism and vested ultimate power in the hands of Shiite clerics.

While all Iranian citizens 15 and older have the right to vote for their leaders, democracy in the country is largely illusory; Iran's constitution guarantees the clerics a firm hold of the reins of power. The country's most influential figure, politically as well as

to work, or even to go out in public without being accompanied by a male relative and being covered from head to toe by a burqa; girls were not permitted to attend school. Men were required to grow beards. The Taliban also banned music, television, and

After toppling Afghanistan's Taliban regime in late 2001, the United States worked with Afghan leaders to build a new government in the war-torn country. (Bottom) Afghani men wait in line to vote in Kabul during an election to select delegates for a constitutional convention. (Inset) As interim president of Afghanistan, Hamid Karzai helped write the constitution that was ratified in January 2004.

movies. Religious police roamed the streets, beating anyone who broke the rules, such as men and women who held hands in public. Many criminals were dealt with more harshly: public amputations and beheadings were a common sight.

The Taliban government also harbored Osama bin Laden, who had established several training camps for Islamic terrorists within Afghanistan's borders. Bin Laden's al-Qaida was implicated in several attacks against U.S. targets, including the August 1998 bombings of the American embassies in Kenya and Tanzania, but the Taliban refused to surrender him to U.S. authorities. Following the al-Qaida-sponsored attacks of September 11, a U.S.-led coalition invaded Afghanistan and toppled the Taliban government. However, bin Laden and Taliban leader Mullah Mohammed Omar eluded capture.

After the fall of the Taliban, a United Nations–sponsored conference was held in Bonn, Germany, where representatives of Afghanistan's leading political groups met to decide on interim steps for governing their country pending the adoption of a new constitution and democratic elections. In June 2002, Hamid Karzai, a leader of one of the Afghan groups, was chosen to be Afghanistan's transitional president. A constitution was written in early 2004, and presidential elections were scheduled to be held by June of that year.

SECULAR VS. RELIGIOUS GOVERNMENTS

More than 98 percent of Turkey's people are Muslims. However, unlike many largely Islamic countries, Turkey has no state religion. In the 1920s the government embraced an official policy of secularism, separating religion from politics. In fact, the Turkish government has restricted certain religious practices. For example, regulations forbade women to cover their heads, a common Islamic custom, while in the workplace or in university classes. In the political realm, members of religious parties were long barred from serving as Turkey's

Index

Picture Credits

3: Brynn Bruijn/Saudi Aramco World/PADIA
8: Corbis Images
12: Katrina Thomas/Saudi Aramco World/PADIA
13: Brand X Pictures
16: S.M. Amin/Saudi Aramco World/PADIA
19: Abdullah Y. Al-Dobais/Saudi Aramco World/PADIA
22: Getty Images
25: Brand X Pictures
28: Tor Eigeland/Saudi Aramco World/PADIA
30: Kevin Bubriski/Saudi Aramco World/PADIA
31: Kevin Bubriski/Saudi Aramco World/PADIA
34: Bibliotheque Nationale, Paris
36: Bibliotheque Nationale, Paris
37: Bibliotheque Nationale, Paris
38: Tor Eigeland/Saudi Aramco World/PADIA
40: Hulton/Archive/Getty Images
43: PhotoDisc
44: PhotoDisc
50: Corbis Images
53: Tor Eigeland/Saudi Aramco World/PADIA

56: S.M. Amin/Saudi Aramco World/PADIA
59: John Feeney/Saudi Aramco World/PADIA
60: (top) IMS Communications, Ltd.; (inset) Robert Azzi/Saudi Aramco World/PADIA
63: Turkish Tourist Office
65: Dick Doughty/Saudi Aramco World/PADIA
69: Dick Doughty/Saudi Aramco World/PADIA
72: Pius Utomi EkpeiAFP/Getty Images
74: IMS Communications, Ltd.
76: Kevin Bubriski Dick Doughty/Saudi Aramco World/PADIA
79: Tauseef MustafaAFP/Getty Images
81: Jewel Samad/AFP/Getty Images
82: Turkish Tourist Office
86: Tor Eigeland/Saudi Aramco World/PADIA
89: Courtesy of the Embassy of Lebanon
90: IMS Communications, Ltd.
93: Corbis Images
96: Henghameh Fahimi/AFP/Getty Images
99: Hulton/Archive/Getty Images
102: Royal Embassy of Saudi Arabia
104: both courtesy U.S. Agency for International Development

Cover: Getty Images; **back cover:** U.S. Agency for International Development

Contributors

General Editor **DR. KHALED ABOU EL FADL** is one of the leading authorities in Islamic law in the United States and Europe. He is currently a visiting professor at Yale Law School as well as Professor of Law at the University of California, Los Angeles (UCLA). He serves on the Board of Directors of Human Rights Watch, and regularly works with various human rights organizations, such as the Lawyer's Committee for Human Rights and Amnesty International. He often serves as an expert witness in international litigation involving Middle Eastern law, and in cases involving terrorism, national security, immigration law and political asylum claims.

Dr. Abou El Fadl's books include *The Place of Tolerance in Islam* (2002); *Conference of the Books: The Search for Beauty in Islam* (2001); *Rebellion in Islamic Law* (2001); *Speaking in God's Name: Islamic Law, Authority, and Women* (2001); and *And God Knows the Soldiers: The Authoritative and Authoritarian in Islamic Discourse* (second edition, revised and expanded, 2001).

Dr. Abou El Fadl was trained in Islamic legal sciences in Egypt, Kuwait, and the United States. After receiving his bachelors degree from Yale University and law degree from the University of Pennsylvania, he clerked for Arizona Supreme Court Justice J. Moeller. While in graduate school at Princeton University, where he earned a Ph.D. in Islamic Law he practiced immigration and investment law in the United States and the Middle East. Before joining the UCLA faculty in 1998, he taught at the University of Texas at Austin, Yale Law School, and Princeton University.

General Editor **DR. SHAMS INATI** is Professor of Islamic Studies at Villanova University. She is a specialist in Islamic philosophy and theology and has published widely in the field. Her publications include *Remarks and Admonitions, Part One: Logic* (1984), *Our Philosophy* (1987), *Ibn Sina and Mysticism* (1996), *The Second Republic of Lebanon* (1999), *The Problem of Evil: Ibn Sina's Theodicy* (2000), and *Iraq: Its History, People, and Politics* (2003). She has also written a large number of articles that have appeared in books, journals, and encyclopedias.

Dr. Inati has been the recipient of a number of awards and honors, including an Andrew Mellon Fellowship, an Endowment for the Humanities grant, a U.S. Department of Defense grant, and a Fulbright grant. For further information about her work, see www.homepage.villanova.edu/shams.inati.

MELISSA S. CARR lives near Nashville, Tennessee. She works as a freelance writer and editor, and also teaches online freshman composition classes for Murray State University in Kentucky, for the University of Tennessee at Martin, and for the University of Phoenix Online. Her interests outside of academia include her dog and her books.